BALD EAGLES!

A MY INCREDIBLE WORLD PICTURE BOOK

MY INCREDIBLE WORLD

The bald eagle is a **bird of prey** found only in North America.

Bald eagles are the national bird and symbol of the United States of America.

They are not actually bald!
They have white feathers
on their head and neck.

Male bald eagles weigh between 7 and 10 pounds (3.2-4.5 kg), while females can weigh up to 14 pounds (6.4 kg)!

They have a wingspan of up to
7 feet (2.1 m), which is about
the width of a small car!

Bald eagles can fly at speeds
of up to 50 miles per hour (80 kph).

They can live up to
30 years in the wild.

Bald eagles are **carnivorous**, eating mainly fish, turtles, and frogs, but they will also eat small mammals and birds.

They have sharp talons that
they use to catch their prey.

Bald eagles mate for life and build large nests together.

Their nests can be up to 13 feet
(4 m) deep and 8 feet (2.4 m) wide!

Bald eagles are **oviparous**, and lay 1 to 3 eggs at a time.

Baby bald eagles are
called **eaglets**.

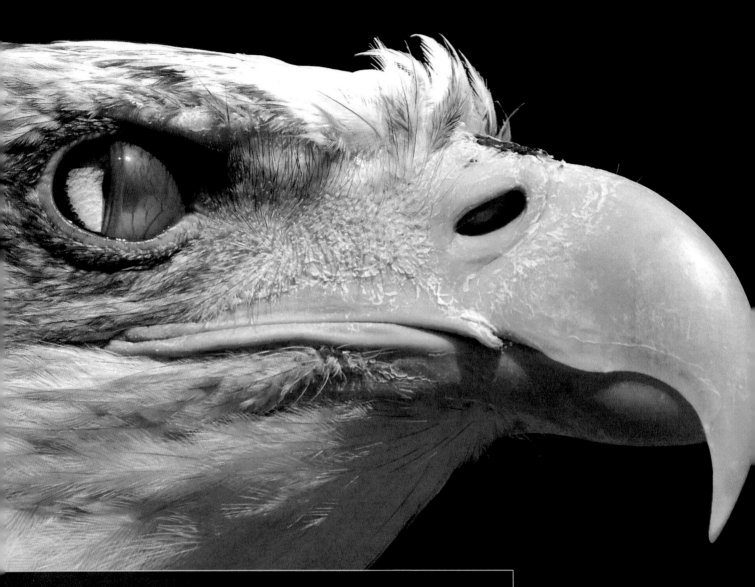

Bald eagles have excellent eyesight and can see prey from over a mile away!

They are also able to see
ultraviolet light, which helps
them find their prey.

Bald eagles are not afraid of water and are excellent swimmers.

They use their wings like
paddles and their tail like
a rudder to help them swim!

Bald eagles have been known
to steal food from other birds
and even from humans!

They are solitary animals and prefer to live alone or in pairs.

Bald eagles are very vocal and have a distinctive high-pitched call.

They are migratory birds, and can travel thousands of miles to find food and breeding grounds.

Bald eagles are incredible!

Made in the USA
Middletown, DE
26 September 2023